The Grandparents Book of Memories

The Grandparents Book of Memories

100 QUESTIONS TO RECALL
THE TIMES OF YOUR LIFE

FOREWORD BY JANE FRANCISCO

HEARST
HOME

foreword

You think you know what a crucial role your mom or dad play in your life, until you have a child — and your parents are suddenly grandparents!

If you're anything like me, when that happens you start to value your time with them in a new way, constantly looking for more opportunities to encourage and strengthen that connection between the generations.

There are few things that have brought me greater joy than seeing my son engage with and learn from my parents — and literally nothing I'm more grateful for than the love they've built together.

I wish I could bottle up the precious moments: from watching my dad demonstrate how to use a yo-yo, to him teaching my son about the challenges and importance of learning to work for your dreams.

Documenting the wisdom, experiences and life lessons for the whole family is priceless, but it often takes a back seat to the urgencies of everyday life. My own grandmother was one of my best friends, but I lost her before I thought to capture her stories and advice for me.

Now is the perfect time to start collecting important memories to inspire your children, your children's children and beyond. Luckily, *The Grandparents Book of Memories* makes it easy to record your wisdom.

Take a walk down memory lane together. You'll cherish the experience of filling the pages with personal reflections, lessons and anecdotes, and the prompts are sure to spark more than a few meaningful conversations. The results, both the memories you relive and the new ones you make, will help the next generation carry on the traditions and legacy of your family.

JANE FRANCISCO
Editor-in-Chief of *Good Housekeeping*

love

Love brings us into the world. For many of us, our first experience of love is the tender care shown to us by parents and grandparents. As we grow, love takes many forms: puppy love and other crushes, deep romantic love, and the astonishing love for our children. Each form of love is different, but all can be equally powerful. It's a privilege to experience any of them and a true gift to get to experience all of them.

{
"To be fully seen by somebody, then,
and be loved anyhow – this is a human offering
that can border on miraculous."
—*Elizabeth Gilbert*
}

Write the names of your great loves along with
a few words that best describe each one.

1.

2.

3.

4.

5.

6.

7.

8.

9.

10.

What are your first memories of your parents?
How did they make you feel loved?

Describe the love you felt for your
children as they grew.

What stunning act of love will
you always remember?

_____

_____

_____

_____

_____

_____

_____

_____

_____

_____

_____

_____

_____

_____

_____

What did it feel like to fall in
love for the first time?

"Where there is love there is life."
—*Mahatma Gandhi*

What's the craziest thing you've
ever done for love?

Who is the love of your life and why?

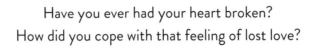

Have you ever had your heart broken?
How did you cope with that feeling of lost love?

What makes your heart feel full?

How do you show appreciation
to the ones you love?

"Love makes your soul crawl out from its hiding place."
—*Zora Neale Hurston*

In what ways do you
treat yourself with compassion?

How do you feel loved by your family?

If someone were to ask, "How do I know if I am really in love?" what would you tell them?

friendship

Friendship sustains us. As we go through life, we enjoy many kinds of friendships. Schoolmates or, later on, workplace friends might be constants by our side until circumstances change; then perhaps after that we keep in touch only occasionally. Other confidants stay with us through the long haul — celebrating milestones, comforting us in hard moments, and serving as our life's witnesses. Last but not least, we can never forget our furry friends, who offer unselfish affection and charming companionship.

{ "Life is partly what we make it, and partly what it is made by the friends we choose." —*Tennessee Williams* }

Write the names of your best friends, along with
a few words that best describe each of them.

1. ....

....

....

2. ....

....

....

3. ....

....

....

4. ....

....

....

5. ....

....

....

6. ....

....

....

7. ....

....

....

8. ....

....

....

9. ....

....

....

10. ....

....

....

Who was your best friend in childhood?

What adventures or mischief did you get into together?

What made you and your friends
laugh in high school?

What gesture of friendship has remained
in your thoughts over the years?

Which special friends attended your wedding or other significant event? Did anyone give a speech or do something memorable during the celebration?

"I awoke this morning with devout thanksgiving
for my friends, the old and the new."

—*Ralph Waldo Emerson*

Did anyone from childhood turn out to
be a lifelong friend? What's one of your greatest
memories together?

Name a friend who helped you when you
were a new parent. How did they support you?

Describe a neighbor you leaned on and
how you supported one another.

How did coworkers, fellow school parents or other
members of your community show up for you?

Was there a trip you took with friends — or an event you shared — that you all talked about for years?

What are your fondest memories
of a beloved family pet?

"Our perfect companions never have
fewer than four feet."
—*Sidonie Gabrielle Colette*

How have you helped friends through the years?
Describe a time you hurried to a friend's side.

How would you encourage others to be a true friend?

wisdom

With age comes wisdom, as Oscar Wilde famously said. Our parents pass down their words of advice and values during childhood, giving us roots. We might follow in their footsteps in some ways, and diverge from other choices to set out on our own path. Early on we may think we know everything, and by middle age we come to understand just how much we have yet to learn and what is truly important to us. As our lives progress, we share our own words of wisdom with the next generation.

{ "It's worth remembering that it is often the small steps, not the giant leaps, that bring about the most lasting change."
—*Queen Elizabeth II* }

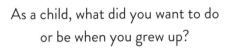

As a child, what did you want to do
or be when you grew up?

When you were young, what did being
"a grown-up" mean to you? When did you feel like
you were finally an adult?

Was there an adult in your early life who
taught you to look at the world differently? What did they
say or do that stuck with you?

As you grew older, did any childhood
beliefs continue to develop or begin to fall away?

How did becoming a parent change you?
What values became more important to you as
you raised your children?

"The days, months and years eventually reveal,
like a Polaroid, a clear picture of how significant events
and decisions ultimately shape our lives."
—*Hoda Kotb*

Did you ever have a mentor?
What do you remember most about them?

What personality trait have you worked
hard to improve or change?

How are you still growing and evolving?

What is one sea change in the world
you've witnessed in your lifetime?

"Do the best you can until you know better.
Then when you know better, do better."
—*Maya Angelou*

What words of wisdom would you
like to be your legacy?

How do you hope the world will evolve
for future generations?

curiosity

Curiosity drives us forward. Isn't it funny what catches our imagination? When we are young we dance or run, play chess or the flute, obsess over dinosaurs or horses. As we grow, our passions may be drawn to other interests that we want to study and carry forward into our adult lives. But then—surprise!—we might pick up new pastimes and hobbies in adulthood, such as gardening, traveling or learning a new language. Curiosity can take us anywhere.

{ "I think, at a child's birth, if a mother could ask a fairy godmother to endow it with the most useful gift, that gift should be curiosity." }
—*Eleanor Roosevelt*

Write the names of our family members, along with a
few words that best describe their talents.

1.

2.

3.

4.

5.

6.

7.

8.

9.

10.

What subject or pursuit has always interested you?

"With curiosity, it has to take a lot of
work to remain ignorant."
—*Benjamin Franklin*

When you were a child, did a family member share a hobby
or interest with you? What do you recall about that?

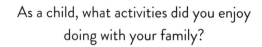

As a child, what activities did you enjoy
doing with your family?

Explain the story behind a favorite family photo
that might make future generations curious. Tuck it into
this book for safekeeping.

In school, what were your favorite subjects and why?

Which school subjects did you find tricky?

What did you study in college or early adulthood?
How did you use what you learned?

What movies, music and books do you enjoy most?

Was there a place you always wanted to visit?
Did you get there?

What activities have you rediscovered
with your own kids or grandkids?

Have your kids or grandkids introduced you to
a new activity or hobby that you enjoy?

"Find something you're passionate about and keep
tremendously interested in it."
—*Julia Child*

Has a new passion brought you joy as an adult?

courage

Courage leads us in a new direction. We're often most proud when we accomplish a goal that initially intimidated us. Overcoming obstacles, whether the demons in our own mind or other challenges, is rewarding. Fearlessness is sometimes about taking heroic action on behalf of others. Or it's about taking small but nerve-jangling risks. Either way, courage is a defining element of our character.

{ "There's something liberating about not pretending. Dare to embarrass yourself. Risk."
—*Drew Barrymore* }

Who is the most courageous person you
know or admire and why?

What took guts to try when you were a child?

Describe a time when you stood up for someone who needed help.

Did one of your family members, friends or neighbors
ever perform a memorable act of courage?

"Stay afraid, but do it anyway. What's important is
the action. You don't have to wait to be confident.
Just do it and eventually the confidence will follow."

—*Carrie Fisher*

What helped you build your self-confidence?

In a situation that requires courage, what strategies
do you use to stay focused and calm?

How does courage help you manage change
and other challenges?

_____

_____

_____

_____

_____

_____

_____

_____

_____

_____

_____

_____

_____

"Twenty years from now you will be more disappointed by
the things that you didn't do than by the ones you did do. So throw
off the bowlines. Sail away from the safe harbor. Catch the trade
winds in your sails. Explore. Dream. Discover."

—*Mark Twain*

Did you take a risk that worked out—with a job,
home, move or another big event?

Did you take a chance that didn't work out?
What did you learn from that?

When have you had to be brave for the sake
of your kids or grandkids?

What's special about your family's heritage, history
or character that makes you proud?

"Success is not final; failure is not fatal:
It is the courage to continue that counts."
—*Winston Churchill*

resilience

Resilience carries us through hard times. Every family has tales of loved ones who displayed grit and determination at a significant point in their lives. Challenging times are inevitable, so cultivating the mindset to endure tough circumstances is important for all of us. Recognizing that strength in yourself and in your family is worth celebrating.

{
"Lessons often come dressed up
as detours and roadblocks."
—*Oprah Winfrey*
}

Do you have a mantra or saying that helps you
through difficult times? When did you first learn it?

Did you experience any tough times during childhood?

"The way I see it, if you want the rainbow,
you gotta put up with the rain."

—*Dolly Parton*

What got you in trouble when you were a child?
What did you learn?

Were you ever teased by siblings or other children?
How did you respond?

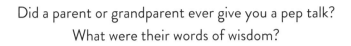

Did a parent or grandparent ever give you a pep talk?
What were their words of wisdom?

Did you ever lose a game or contest
that was important to you? How did you learn
to be a good sport?

What's an example of you or your family making the
best of an unfortunate situation?

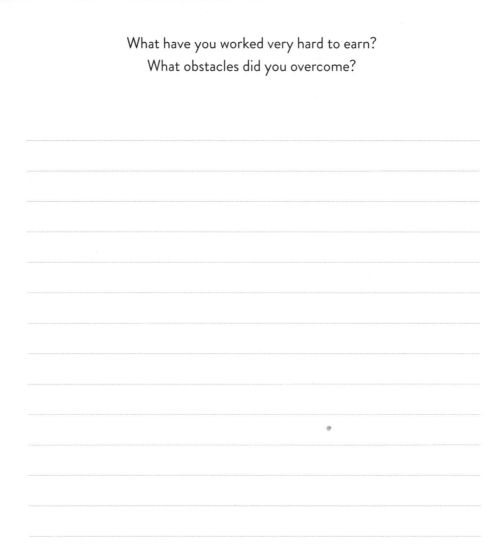

What have you worked very hard to earn?
What obstacles did you overcome?

"So often in life, things that you regard as an
impediment turn out to be great, good fortune."
—*Ruth Bader Ginsburg*

What skill or accomplishment did you develop
that still makes you feel proud?

How have you helped a child or
grandchild overcome an obstacle?

Have you dealt with the bad times in a way that makes
you feel proud when you look back?

rituals

Rituals bind us to our loved ones. Families share traditions that create a profound feeling of belonging. Whether it's how you celebrate a holiday or end a phone call, every family has special and personal routines. It's rewarding to pass down time-tested rituals and thrilling to watch the next generation create new ones. Sometimes old customs fade away, and that's okay. Our practices served their purpose, and then we invent wonderful new ones.

{ "Remember to celebrate milestones as
you prepare for the road ahead."
—*Nelson Mandela* }

What's your favorite holiday and why?

What foods did you have as a child that will
always remind you of family?

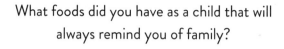

_____

_____

_____

_____

_____

_____

_____

_____

_____

_____

_____

"Time flies over us but leaves its shadow behind."
—*Nathaniel Hawthorne*

How do you recall and appreciate memories of your
own parents or other older relatives?

Is there a family custom from the old days that
you were happy to see fade away?

What new traditions have you started
with your kids or grandkids?

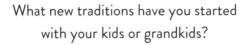

What books did
you love to read to
your kids?

What songs did
you sing to them?

1.

2.

3.

4.

5.

1.

2.

3.

4.

5.

What songs transport you to a specific
time or event in your life?

Did you try to instill a sense of spirituality
in your children? How so?

Describe an object that holds
sentimental value for you.

"The sacred is not in heaven or far away. It is all around us,
and small human rituals can connect us to its presence. And of course, the
greatest challenge (and gift) is to see the sacred in each other."

–Alma Luz Villanueva

Do you have any superstitions or objects
that you hope bring good luck?

What place is special to you and your family—a vacation spot,
or a town where previous generations lived?

How did your parents acknowledge and celebrate
your family's culture or history?

What's one family tradition that you would love
to see continue in the generations ahead?

happiness

Happiness enriches us. Our search for joy leads us along with hope and optimism. Children find happiness everywhere. As we grow a bit older, we might look for thrills from exciting, new experiences. As we come into our later years, we might come to understand that every-day blessings and the simple company of friends and family give us a profound sense of well-being, just as fulfilling as any big adventure.

{
"Happiness often sneaks in through a door
you didn't know you left open."

—*John Barrymore*
}

Describe a happy time in your life.

What sparked joy when you were a child?

What makes you laugh?

What made your mom or dad happy?

What place has always made you feel happy?

Which friend or relative could always cheer you up?

"We all live with the objective of being happy; our lives are different and yet the same."

—*Anne Frank*

What are the ingredients for "a happy home"?

What did you do to help make your own children happy?

What makes your spouse or partner happy?

What simple pleasure do you enjoy today?

How do you try to pass happiness on to others?

"Don't count the days; make the days count."
—*Muhammad Ali*

What does happiness mean to you?

What's your recipe for finding happiness every day?

gratitude

Gratitude fills us with peace. Life brings us many moments to treasure: good times with friends, new marriages and newborns, the turn of the seasons. Reflecting daily on what you are grateful for and writing down what you feel can offer pleasure and clarity about what's truly important to you.

{ "When I started counting my blessings, my whole life turned around." —*Willie Nelson* }

When you count your blessings,
what comes to mind first?

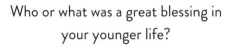

Who or what was a great blessing in
your younger life?

"As we express our gratitude, we must
never forget that the highest appreciation is not
to utter words but to live by them."
—*John F. Kennedy*

What teacher or mentor do you wish you could go back
and thank? What would you say?

What's the most important lesson that
a parent or mentor taught you?

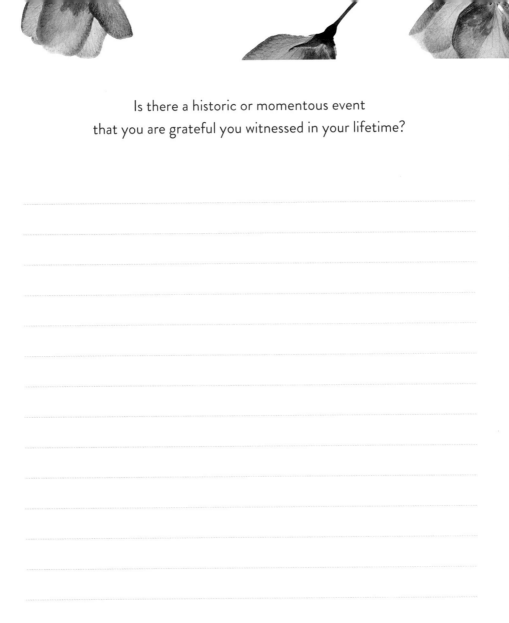

Is there a historic or momentous event
that you are grateful you witnessed in your lifetime?

"When I'm worried and I can't sleep,
I count my blessings instead of sheep."

—*Irving Berlin*

Did you ever experience "a blessing in disguise"
or an answered prayer?

Have you supported a charity or a cause because you are grateful for their work?

Did you ever do volunteer work?
How did your contribution feel meaningful?

"Gratitude is a divine emotion: It fills the heart, but not to
bursting; it warms it, but not to fever."
—*Charlotte Brontë*

What qualities are you grateful to see in
your kids and grandkids?

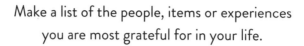

Make a list of the people, items or experiences
you are most grateful for in your life.

1. ....
   ....
   ....

2. ....
   ....
   ....

3. ....
   ....
   ....

4. ....
   ....
   ....

5. ....
   ....
   ....

6. ....
   ....
   ....

7. ....
   ....
   ....

8. ....
   ....
   ....

9. ....
   ....
   ....

10. ....
    ....
    ....

11.

12.

13.

14.

15.

16.

17.

18.

19.

20.

Write a letter to the next generation expressing
your gratitude and wisdom.

HEARST
HOME

Copyright © 2023 by Hearst Magazine Media, Inc.

All rights reserved. The written instructions in this volume are intended for
the personal use of the reader and may be reproduced for that purpose only.
Any other use, especially commercial use, is forbidden under law without the
written permission of the copyright holder.

Text by Jessica Hartshorn
Cover and book design by Kristen Male
Images on pages 4-9, 50-64, 66-67, 69-75, 88-102 and 104-128 from
Shutterstock. All other images from Getty Images.

Library of Congress Cataloging-in-Publication Data Available on request

10 9 8 7 6 5 4 3 2 1

Published by Hearst Home, an imprint of
Hearst Books/Hearst Communications, Inc.

Hearst Communications, Inc.
300 W. 57th Street
New York, NY 10019

Hearst Home, the Hearst Home logo, and Hearst Books are registered
trademarks of Hearst Communications, Inc.

For information about custom editions, special sales, premium and corporate
purchases: hearst.com/magazines/hearst-books

Printed in China
ISBN 978-1-950785-94-0